Glide Into Winter
With Math and Science

EDITORS

Arthur Wiebe
Project Director
Fresno Pacific College

Larry Ecklund
Project Director
Fresno Pacific College

Judith Hillen
Associate Project Director
Fresno Pacific College

WRITING TEAM

Robin Adair
First Grade Teacher
Fresno Unified School District
Fresno, California

Jill Ewing
First Grade Teacher
Madera Unified School District
Madera, California

Shirley Faircloth
Kindergarten Teacher
Central Union School District
Stratford, California

Janice Nikoghosian
Kindergarten/First Grade Teacher
Hanford Elementary School District
Hanford, California

Cynthia Peterson
First Grade Teacher
Turlock Christian School
Turlock, California

Darlene Smith
Kindergarten/First Grade Teacher
Fresno Unified School District
Fresno, California

Sheila Wiebe
First Grade Teacher
Kings Canyon Unified School District
Reedley, California

FACILITATORS

Sheryl Mercier
Sixth Grade Teacher
Lemoore Elementary School District
Lemoore, California

Nancy Norsworthy
First Grade Teacher
Nevada City Elementary School
Nevada City, California

ILLUSTRATIONS

by

Sheryl Mercier

AIMS (Activities Integrating Mathematics and Science) began in 1981 with a grant from the National Science Foundation. The non-profit AIMS Education Foundation publishes hands-on instructional materials (books and the monthly AIMS Newsletter) that integrate curricular disciplines such as mathematics, science, language arts, and social studies. The Foundation sponsors a national program of professional development through which educators may gain both an understanding of the AIMS philosophy and expertise in teaching by integrated, hands-on methods.

ISBN 1-881431-17-7

Printed in the United States of America

Table of Contents

Index of Skills

MATH SKILLS

SCIENCE PROCESSES

I HEAR, AND I FORGET
I SEE, AND I REMEMBER
I DO, AND I UNDERSTAND

–Chinese Proverb

Introduction

Whether you are amidst the rain, fog, or snow, here is a remedy for those cold winter blues! Winterize with math and science! The winter booklet of the Project AIMS K-1 series is here to dispel those feelings of winter.

The Project AIMS series for K-1 is seasonally based to make it convenient for you to incorporate these investigations into your present curriculum. Because of the peak learning experiences you will be presenting to your students, they will feel like winners when it comes to math and science.

This series is not designed with a specific scope and sequence where each succeeding lesson is based on the preceding lesson. The investigations are written in such a way that your students will discover the true meaning of math and science integration—application of knowledge in the real world.

The Project AIMS K-1 series allows for flexibility for usage in your classroom. Use your own judgment to find the appropriate application and extension of each investigation. Each activity comes complete with a student activity page that you may wish to send home with your students or start a math-science scrap book.

This booklet is not intended to replace your science program, but rather it is intended to enhance it. Remember that these experiences place prime emphasis on the science processes and appropriate math skills. It is not necessary to have a laboratory and elaborate equipment to run a strong science program. All that is needed is every day materials and your willingness to try new ideas!

—The K-1 Series Writing Team

Catch Me... If You Can

I. **Topic Area**
Foods

II. **Introductory Statement**
Students will learn how to make gingerbread and form it into a life size gingerbread man.

III. **Key Question**
How could we make a life-size gingerbread man of our very own?

IV. **Math Skills**
a. Applying formulas
b. Counting
c. Equations
d. Fractions
e. Measuring
f. Patterns
g. Ratios
h. Timing

Science Processes
a. Measuring
b. Controlling variables
c. Interpreting data

V. **Materials**
- ½ cup soft margarine
- 1½ cups brown sugar (packed)
- 2¼ cups molasses
- 1 cup cold water
- 10½ cups flour
- 3 teaspoons baking soda
- 1½ teaspoons salt
- 1½ teaspoons allspice
- 1½ teaspoons ginger
- 1½ teaspoons cloves
- 1½ teaspoons cinnamon
- butcher paper
- cookie sheets
- rolling pin
- knife
- spatula
- mixing bowl
- measuring cups and spoons
- decorations for cooked gingerbread: raisins nuts, candy, colored frostings, etc.

VI. **Background Information**
Gingerbread Recipe
Mix: ½ cup soft margarine
     1½ cups brown sugar (packed)
     2¼ cups molasses
Stir in: 1 cup cold water
Sift together and add to mixture:
     10½ cups flour
     3 teaspoons baking soda
     1½ teaspoons salt
     1½ teaspoons allspice
     1½ teaspoons ginger
     1½ teaspoons cloves
     1½ teaspoons cinnamon
Roll dough 3/8 inch thick and cut into body parts using pattern.
Bake in 350° oven 12-15 minutes (lightly greased pan)
Decorate

VII. **Management**
1. This activity should be broken into 3 separate sessions:
   a. Session One—tracing of a child's body onto butcher paper for a cookie pattern
   b. Session Two—making the gingerbread dough
   c. Session Three—decorating the giant cookie after it has been cooked.
2. All three sessions are best conducted in small groups of 4-5 children.

VIII. **Advanced Preparation**
1. Have butcher paper ready for tracing.
2. Purchase all the ingredients necessary for the gingerbread dough and decorations.

IX. Procedure

1. Session One:

Select the student to serve as the pattern for the gingerbread man. Have the child lie on the butcher paper while the teacher traces around his or her body. Cut out the figure and save for the second session.

2. Session Two:

Measure and mix all the ingredients into a large bowl. Refrigerate the dough for 2-3 hours. Roll dough 3/8 inch thick on a floured table. Cut the body pattern into assorted body sections—be sure each piece will be able to fit on the cookie sheets. Place the pattern pieces on the dough and cut out. Bake each section accordingly.

3. Session Three:

Working in small groups, decorate each body section with nuts, raisins, candy, and frosting. Reassemble the gingerbread man and check for symmetry or the patterns. You might like to arrange your gingerbread man on a sturdy piece of cardboard so it can be moved for display. Using extra frosting, "glue" each piece of your cookie to the selected piece of cardboard.

X. Discussion

1. Why is this recipe called gingerbread? What other ingredients did we use?
2. What would happen if we didn't read the recipe carefully and used whatever amount of each ingredient we wanted?
3. What else could we make with our cookie dough?

XI. Extensions

After baking the cookie pieces, hide them somewhere in the room. Explain to the children that when you opened the oven to check the gingerbread man, he jumped out and ran away. Suggest hunting for him and conduct a school-wide hunt. While the children are out of the room, have another adult reassemble the giant cookie. When the children are ready to give up their search, return to the room. The gingergread man will have returned. You might want to do this extension after decorating your gingerbread man.

XII. Curriculum Coordinates

Language Arts

1. Have the children write their own gingerbread man stories, explaining who would chase them and how they would escape.

Art

1. Using "goofy goop" decorate individual construction paper gingerbread men.

Goofy Goop

3 cups flour
3 cups salt
3 cups water

Separate the goop into individual squeeze bottles and add colored tempera paint. Use this to decorate construction paper gingerbread men.

GLIDE INTO WINTER

Catch me if you can!

GLIDE INTO WINTER

GLIDE INTO WINTER

© 1987 AIMS Education Foundation

How Does Your Corn Pop?

I. Topic Area
Food (Popcorn)

II. Introductory Statement
Students will listen for evidence that popcorn is popping and guess how far it will travel from the popper.

III. Key Question
When the popcorn begins to pop how far do you think it will go?

IV. Math Skills

a. Estimating	
b. Predicting	
c. Measuring length	
d. Graphing	
1. Counting	
2. Recording data	

Science Processes
a. Observing
b. Estimating
c. Interpreting data
d. Applying and generalizing

V. Materials
- Popcorn popper, electric (air blower type)
- Popcorn
- Milk cartons (½ gallon) cut and made into cubes for each child
- Paper for predicting distance to be placed by the popper
- Graph for predicting distance popcorn will pop

VII. Management
This activity will take 20-30 minutes. It may be done in a whole class setting.

VIII. Advanced Preparation
On paper approximately 24″ × 36″, section the paper into 5-6 strips. Make each section a different color and design. Place this paper in front of the electric popper.

Graph
On paper approximately 12′ × 36″ put the color coding at the top of the paper to match the color coding on the predicting paper. Cubes will be placed on the graph for comparisons.

Milk carton cubes
Use ½ gallon milk cartons, two for each child. Cut 4″ from the bottom. Push the two cartons together, open end to open end. Cover with contact paper. Using a 3″ square paper write each child's name on a square and tape one name on each cube. A child's picture can also be used.

IX. Procedure
1. Show the children the popcorn popper and discuss what it is and what it will do.
2. Discuss the unpopped kernels and talk about what will happen to them when they are popped; size change, color change, smell, etc.
3. Discuss what makes the kernels change.
4. Tell the children that you are going to put the popcorn into the popper and they are going to predict how far the kernels will pop out of the popper. You will place the paper with the colored strips for predicting by the popper.
5. Students will make their predictions, one at a time, and the teacher will mark on the paper what each child's prediction is.
6. Mark on the paper with an "X" the spot each child chooses. Then each child places his/her milk carton cube on the graph by matching the color on the prediction paper.
7. Discuss where all the predictions are on the paper. Compare lengths; longest, shortest, etc. Discuss the graph and compare which color has the most, fewest, etc.
8. Plug in the popper and put in the popcorn. Students observe what happens and watch as the popcorn lands on the paper. Compare where the popcorn lands and how well the students predicted. Which children made the most accurate predictions? Discuss the graph and decide how many estimated the correct color the kernel that pop the farthest.

X. Discussion
1. What made the popcorn pop?
2. How far away was the farthest kernel?
3. How far away was the closest kernel?
4. How many children made good predictions? Why were they good predictions?
5. If we did the same lesson again would the popcorn pop the same distances?

XI. Extensions

1. Do an estimating lesson on the number of unpopped kernels in a jar. Then estimate again on the number of popped kernels in a jar. Which jar has the most? Why?

2. Bring a bag of popped corn. Students can estimate how many kernels of popped corn are in the bag. Use different measurement devices to guess how many, such as, how many styrofoam cups full are in the bag? How many pie plates full are in the bag? Cereal bowls? etc.

3. Have the students estimate the kernels of popcorn needed to completely cover the surface of a paper plate, a length of roving, a sheet of 5×7 paper, etc.

XII. Curriculum Coordinates

Language Arts

1. Brainstorm words to describe the *sounds* of popcorn popping. The teacher should record these on the chalkboard (bang, pop, sizzle, etc.). Brainstorm words that describe the *looks* (white, fluffy, like a cloud, etc.). *Smell* the popcorn. Repeat the brainstorming process. Students should *feel* and *taste* the popcorn and repeat the same process.

2. Play the Popcorn Game for reinforcement of skills.

3. Read Popcorn poem for the flannel board.

Art

1. Dye popcorn with powdered tempera and create Spring pictures with blossoms, Spring mosaics, pussy willows, etc. Put the popcorn in a plastic bag and sprinkle the powdered tempera over it. Shake the bag until the popcorn is coated.

Science

1. Using a hot plate, heat water in a pan. Place a soda bottle in the hot water and attach a balloon to the top of the bottle. Let the children see how heat rises and expands and watch the balloon fill with heated air. Then place the bottle in cool water and let the children compare what happens. How can you relate this to the popcorn?

Social Studies

1. When you take a walk to the park, feed the ducks popcorn.

2. For a farm unit, make a lamb or sheep using popcorn to represent the wool.

Popcorn Game

One popper per player. "Popcorn" is placed in central box or pile. Players draw and name whatever is written on "popcorn," or use with task cards and blank popcorn.

Child with the most popcorn in his "popper" is declared the winner.

Suggested uses: Letters, Numbers, Combinations, Number Facts, Roman Numerals, Time, Money, etc.

Popcorn Story

Ten white kernels of corn to pop.
Watch them dance as they get hot!

Count as each bursts from its narrow pen:
One, two, three, four, five, six, seven, eight, nine, ten.

Tommy ate one; it tasted fine,
But then there were only nine.

Billy ate another; it tasted great,
But alas, that left only eight.

The next one was eaten by Kevin,
And then there were only seven.

Len Choo ate his with chopsticks,
And then there were only six.

George went for his with a dive,
And then what was left? Only five.

Patty ate hers and wanted more,
But then there remained just four.

Jill ate hers faster than you could see.
And then there were only three.

Dina said, "More," when she was through,
But then there were only two.

Joanna ate one just for fun,
And there was only one.

Jenny ate the very last one,
And that meant that there were none.

How Does Your Corn Pop?

1. On paper approximately 24"x36", section the paper into 5 or 6 strips.
2. Make each paper a different color or design.
3. Place the paper in front of the electric popper.

(Mark an X on the spot each child predicts a popcorn will land.)

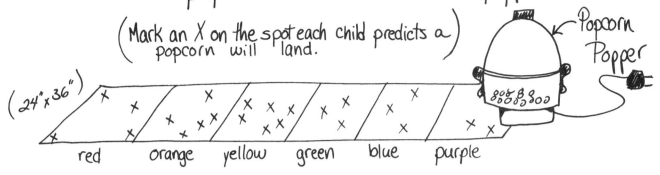

red   orange   yellow   green   blue   purple

Prediction Cubes

1. Use ½ gallon milk cartons - 2 per child. Cut 4" from the bottom to form squares.

2. Push the 2 cartons together, open end to open end to form a cube

3. Cover with contact paper.

Attach a name, photo or picture drawing of each child.

Jane

Graph

On paper approximately 12"x36", put the color coding to match the coding by the popcorn popper predicting paper. Place the graph on the wall or floor. Each child places his cube on, or by, the color that matches his prediction X.

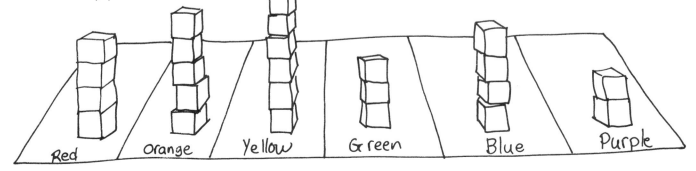

Red   Orange   Yellow   Green   Blue   Purple

Popcorn Game

9

Glue popcorn or cotton here.

If the Shoe Fits...

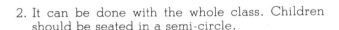

I. Topic Area
Sorting by attributes

II. Introductory Statement
Students will be able to identify the attribute by which shoes are being sorted.

III. Key Question
Can you determine into which group your shoe will be sorted?

IV. Math Skills
a. Predicting
b. Logical thinking
c. Observing
d. Generalizing
e. Attributes

Science Processes
a. Observing and classifying
b. Interpreting data
c. Applying and Generalizing

V. Materials
- One "yes" card for each child in the group, plus 2 more
- One "no" card for each child in the group, plus 2 more
- A defined area for sorting, such as a hula hoop, a large piece of paper, a space on the floor or carpet, etc.
- Elf (see elf pattern)

VI. Background Information
This activity was designed to be used in December. Before beginning the lesson, read or tell the story "The Elves and the Shoemaker." This activity could also be used in March with a leprechaun replacing the elf.

VII. Management
1. Allow at least 30 minutes for each sorting and discussion period. The shoes should be sorted only one way each time, although this activity may be repeated several times.
2. It can be done with the whole class. Children should be seated in a semi-circle.

VIII. Advanced Preparation
1. Prepare one "yes" and one "no" prediction card for each child. You will also need to prepare two more sets; one to be used by the teacher and the other to be used in the sorting area. Cards can be made by using 3" × 5" index cards or tagboard cut to size. Print "yes" on *both* sides of one set of cards and print "no" on both sides of the other set of cards. (If children are non-readers, it may be easier for them to distinguish between the two words if the words are printed in different colors.)
2. Make a copy of the elf to use when introducing the lesson.
3. Read or tell the story "The Elves and the Shoemaker."
4. Have a defined area for sorting. Place a "yes" card and the elf at the top of one area, and place the "no" card to the side of it. (For example, the elf and the "yes" card might be placed inside a hula hoop or a yarn circle and the "no" card could be placed just to the side of the circle.
5. Decide which attribute will be used in sorting the shoes. (Some suggestions: shoelaces, velcro snaps, smooth soles, color, etc.)

IX. Procedure

1. Have the students take off their shoes and sit in a semi-circle around the sorting area. The children should put their shoes next to them.

2. Pass out the "yes" and "no" cards. Make sure the children can tell which card says yes and which says no.

3. Tell the students that most elves are like the ones in the story "The Elves and the Shoemaker;" they like to *make* shoes but that this elf (indicate elf in sorting area) likes to *take* shoes. Ask, "Do you think you can guess which shoes he'd like to take today?" Explain to the children that they will be using the cards to show their answers: If they think the elf will take a shoe, they hold up the "yes" card. If they don't think he'll take it, they should hold up the "no" card.

4. Choose a child to hold up his or her shoe so that everyone can see it. Ask, "Do you think the elf will take this shoe today?" Children should respond by holding up the card of their choice.

5. The child with the shoe checks the responses and starts to put the shoe in either the "yes" or the "no" sorting area. Before putting the shoe down, the child and the rest of the class check with the teacher who then holds up the correct card. The child then places the shoe in the sorting area. Continue giving turns until all the children have had an opportunity to sort one shoe.

X. Discussion

1. Why did the elf decide to take these shoes today? (Indicate "yes" area.) What is the same about all of these shoes?

2. Were you able to predict which ones he'd take?

3. Why didn't he take these? (Indicate "no" area.)

XI. Extensions

1. Repeat this activity several times using a different attribute each time.

2. Sort other objects by attribute.

3. Repeat the shoe sorting activity but have a student determine the attribute and have him or her take the teacher's place.

XII. Curriculum Coordinates

Language Arts

1. Make 5 copies of the elf pattern and make stick puppets. Use them with the poem "Five Little Elves."

2. Ask the children to decide if they would like to be an elf who makes shoes or one who takes shoes? Why?

3. The "yes" and "no" cards can be used for answering reading comprehension questions.

4. Have the children think of words that describe shoes.

5. Teach the nursery rhyme "There Was An Old Lady Who Lived in a Shoe."

Art

1. What can you make from a shoe shape? Have students trace their shoes onto construction paper and cut it out. By adding details made from paper, crayons and other materials, have the children see what they can make from that shape.

2. Make a shoe collage.

Physical Education

1. Have shoe relays.

13

Five Little Elves

Five little elves came to visit today,
And this is what I heard them say:
The first one said, "I like to play."
The second one said, "Lets hide away."
The third one said," Lets hide in_____'s shoe!"
The fourth one said, "But there's only room for two."
The fifth one said, "Then we'll need some more!"
So they took all your shoes and they ran out the door!

by Janice Nikoghosian
©1984

14

Colorful Crystal Garden

I. **Topic Area**
   Growing Crystals

II. **Introductory Statement**
   Students will "grow" crystals.

III. **Key Question**
   "How can we grow crystals?"

IV. **Math Skills**
   a. Formula
   b. Measuring volume
   c. Attributes

   Science Processes
   a. Observing and classifying
   b. Measuring
   c. Controlling variables

V. **Materials**
   - six charcoal briquets
   - disposable aluminum pie tin
   - liquid bluing
   - table salt
   - clear ammonia
   - water
   - measuring spoons
   - coffee can with lid
   - liquid food coloring in four colors

VI. **Background Information**
   1. Students should understand what the term "crystal" means and should be shown samples of crystals such as quartz or salt.
   2. Natural crystals were formed when the earth cooled down millions of years ago.
   3. It will take longe for crystals to form during the wintertime.
   4. The Crystal Garden will have the appearance of coral and will be soft and powdery to the touch.

VII. **Management**
   1. This activity may take twenty minutes.
   2. New crystals will begin to form within twenty-four hours.

VIII. **Advanced Procedure**
   1. Have all materials out and ready to be used.

IX. **Procedure**
   1. Ask: "What will happen if we mix these ingredients (salt, bluing, ammonia, food coloring, water, charcoal briquets) together?"
   2. Write down the students' responses on the chalkboard or on a piece of butcher paper.
   Example: "It will turn colors."
   "It will dry up."

3. Tell the students they will find out what will happen by assisting you in the following procedure:
   a. Place six charcoal briquets in the aluminum pie tin.
   b. Measure 6 tsp. of salt, 6 Tbs. of bluing, 6 Tbs. of water, and 1 Tbs. of ammonia. Pour all ingredients into a coffee can. Mix them well.
   c. Squeeze different food colors onto four of the briquets—one color for each briquet. Squeeze all four colors on the fifth briquet. The sixth briquet is not to be colored.
   d. Pour the salt mixture evenly over the six briquets.
   e. Place the pie tin and briquets in a warm place.
   f. Mix the same solution of salt, bluing, ammonia, and water in the can and cover tightly.
   g. Add this solution over the "garden" of briquets every day to keep the crystals growing. Add the food coloring every two days.
4. Have the students describe what the crystals look like each day for eight days (color, size, shape, texture). Record responses on the chalkboard or on a piece of butcher paper.

X. **Discussion**
   1. Compare what the students thought would happen to what actually happened with the briquets and solution.
   2. Can anyone think of other types of crystals? (diamonds, salt, quartz)
   3. Are any of these crystals valuable?
   4. Can you bring a crystal into the classroom?

XI. **Extensions**
   1. Make sugar rock candy.
   2. Give every child a crystal of their very own (really a piece of "rock" salt) to take home!
   3. Using the student page, have the children color a "before" and "after" picture of the charcoal briquets.

XII. **Curriculum Coordinates**
   Language Arts
   1. Read "The Dark Crystal"
   2. Let the children look through a kaleidoscope and tell what colors and shapes they see.

   Art
   1. Make a mosaic using colored chips of paper on a black background.
   2. Make a collage of crushed, dyed eggshells.

Crystal Garden

I. Place 6 charcoal briquets in an aluminum pie tin.

II. Measure 6 tsp. salt, 6 tbs. of bluing, 6 tbs. of water and 1 tbs. of ammonia. Pour into a coffee can. Mix them well.

III. Squeeze different food colors onto 4 of the briquets ··· one color for each. Squeeze all 4 colors on the fifth briquet. The sixth is not to be colored.

IV. Pour the salt mixture evenly over the 6 briquets.

V. Place the pie tin and briquets in a warm place.

VI. Mix the same solution of salt bluing, ammonia and water in the can and cover tightly.

VII. Add this solution over the "garden" of briquets every day to keep the crystals growing. Add the food coloring every 2 days.

IX. Have the students describe what the crystals look like every day for eight days (color, size, shape, texture). Record responses on the chalkboard or on butcher paper.

The Crystal Garden will have the appearance of coral and will be soft and powdery to the touch.

Crystal Gardens

Before

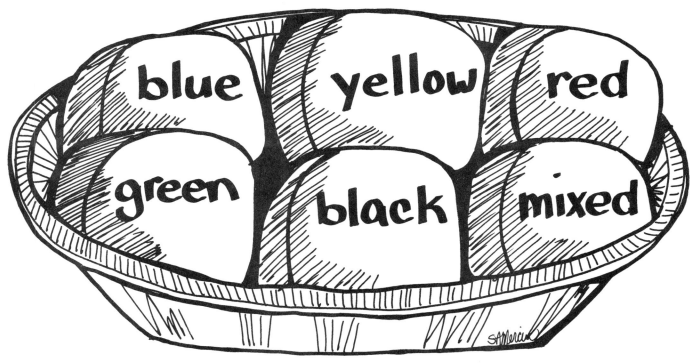

blue   yellow   red

green   black   mixed

After

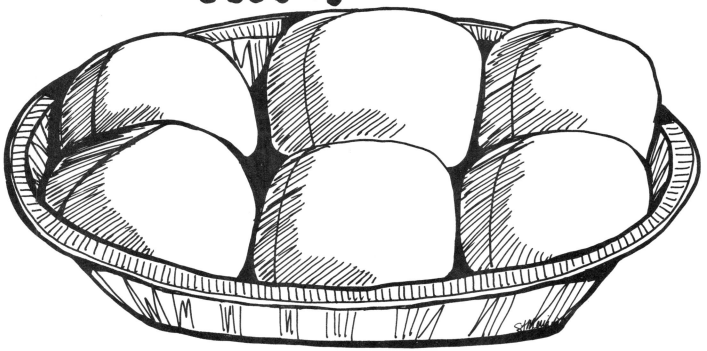

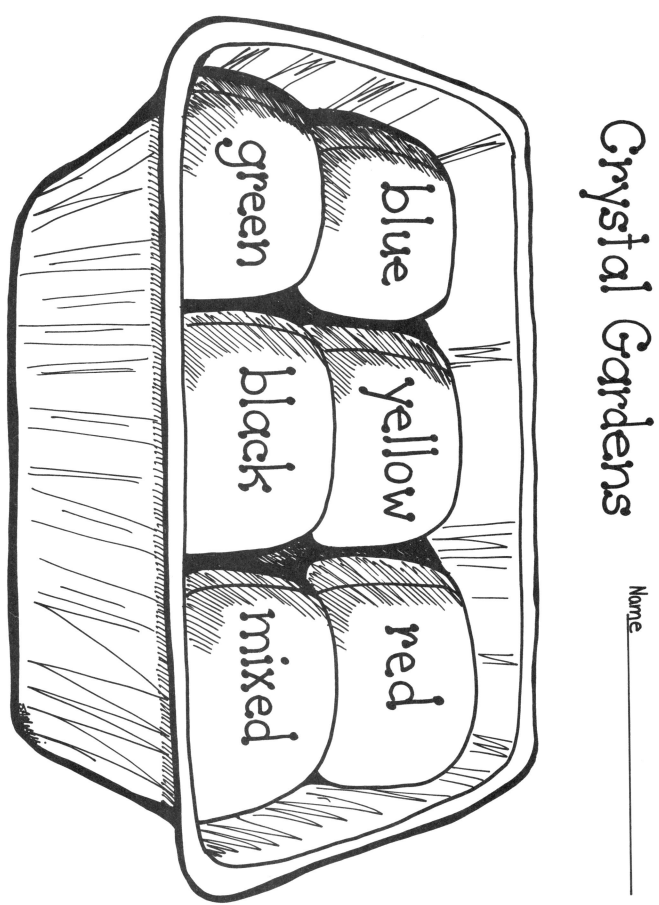

Crystal Gardens

Name _____

Polar Bear Pie

I. Topic Area
Food/Weather/Winter

II. Introductory Statement
Students will predict how long it will take the Eskimo Pie to melt. Students will also estimate how many bites it will take to eat the Eskimo Pie.

III. Key Question
How long will it take for the Eskimo Pie to melt?

IV. Math Skills
a. Graphing
b. Recording data
c. Interpreting data
d. Counting
e. Patterning
f. Estimating
g. Measuring

Science Processes
a. Observing
b. Measuring
c. Gathering and recording data
d. Predicting
e. Interpreting data

V. Materials
- graphs
- paper towels
- Eskimo Pies—one for each student
- worksheet
- construction paper strips for patterns
- toothpicks

VII. Management
1. This activity will take about 45 minutes when done inside a classroom.
2. This activity can get a little sticky, so you may want to be near some water.
3. You may want to keep the Eskimo Pie on ice or in a cooler while you are doing the graphing activity.

VIII. Advanced Preparation
1. Two graphs are needed for these activities. One can be a bar graph, and one may be a chart to simply record their estimates on.

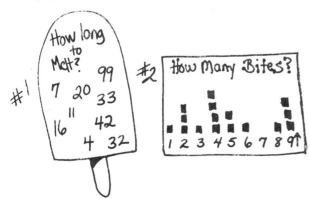

2. Cut strips of dark colored construction or butcher paper about 4" × 18". These will be used for the pattern strip of mini-ice cream sticks (tooth picks).

IX. Procedure
1. Bring out one Eskimo Pie and ask the students to estimate how many minutes it will take for the Eskimo Pie to melt. Record the predictions.
2. Set the Eskimo Pie out on a plate and start the timing. Check the progress every 5-10 minutes. You may want to record observations of the changes that take place while melting.
3. While you are waiting for it to melt down (which will take between 30-45 minutes), have the students predict how many bites it would take them to eat an Eskimo Pie of their own. Record the predictions on a graph and discuss.
4. Pass one out to each child with a paper towel and a piece of scrap paper to make tally marks, so they don't lose count.
5. While still waiting, pass out the toothpicks and the strips of paper for their own pattern strip.
6. Pass out the worksheet at the end of this lesson to the children to work on and take home to show their parents.
7. If you are still waiting, the children can wash off their used sticks and use them to find objects that are longer and/or the same length. This could be used as a homework assignment too.

X. Discussion
1. What would make the pie melt faster? slower?
2. What other objects would melt faster or slower than an Eskimo Pie?

XI. Extensions
1. How many sticks long are you?
2. How many sticks will balance a _____?
3. Run the Eskimo Pie worksheet on different colors of construction paper to make a pattern on a 5" × 36" strip of butcher paper.

XII. Curriculum Coordinates
Language Arts
1. Write and/or draw pictures for the directions for making an Eskimo Pie.
2. Invent your own frozen treat. What would it be? How would it look? What is its name?
3. Find and read stories about eskimos.

Music
1. Use the sticks to tap out patterns or rythms on desks, chairs, floors, windows, etc.

Cooking
1. Make homemade ice cream in the classroom. Use your favorite recipe!

Polar Bear Pie

1. I think I can eat my pie in ___ bites.

2. My polar bear pie is as cold as _____.

3. The ice cream is as white as _____.

4. The sun is as warm as _____.

5. The chocolate is as brown as _____.

6 The stick is as long as _____.

Trace your stick here.

7. I ate my polar bear pie in ___ bites.

GLIDE INTO WINTER

© 1987 AIMS Education Foundation

Goober Peas

I. Topic Area
Food

II. Introductory Statement
Students will learn what a goober pea is.

III. Key Question
Now that you have your goober pea, how many nuts do you think are inside?

IV. Math Skills

Math Skills
- a. Graphing
  1. Recording data
  2. Interpreting data
  3. Counting
- b. Estimating
- c. Patterning
- d. Applying a formula

Science Processes
- a. Observing
- b. Estimating
- c. Gathering and recording data
- d. Interpreting data

V. Materials
- blender
- spatula
- 1 measuring cup for each group
- 1 stalk of celery for each child
- butcher paper for a graph approximately 24" × 36"
- 1 brown and 1 yellow square of construction paper for each child
- a copy of pattern sheet #1 run on brown construction paper for each child
- a strip of construction paper or butcher paper (approximately 24" × 4") for peanut pattern
- 2 lb. bag of peanuts in shells
- 1 knife for each group

VI. Background Information
1. This activity takes two days and the Advanced Preparation and Procedure are listed separately for each day.
2. Goober Peas are peanuts.
3. Peanuts are from the pea family.
4. Peanuts grow under the ground and need to be planted each year.
5. Peanuts are grown in places with warm climates with sandy soil.

6. *Peanut Butter Recipe* (a double recipe is needed for 25 or more children)
   1½ cups of shelled peanuts yield ¾ of a cup of peanut butter.
   Put 1½ cups of shelled peanuts in the blender. Turn the blender on the highest speed and let it run for several minutes. Stop the blender occasionally to scrape the sides of the blender and around the blades with the spatula. It will take about 5 minutes to start creaming. Continue to blend until the peanut butter is the consistency you prefer. Repeat the procedure again for the second batch of peanuts.

VII. Management
1. This activity will take 2 days for about 30 minutes each day.
2. You'll need an area where you can safely use a blender.
3. Work in small groups. Each group will need a measuring cup for the shelled peanuts. Since the doubled recipe calls for 3 cups of shelled peanuts, you may want 3 groups, each filling a 1 cup measuring cup.

VIII. Advanced Preparation—*Day One*
1. Gather books and pictures of peanuts.
2. Prepare the graph and squares for recording. An example might be:
   a. Yellow □'s in one column for the child's estimate.
   b. Using brown paper, children would draw and cut out a nut shape to be placed in the appropriate column to show the actual number of peanuts in the shell.

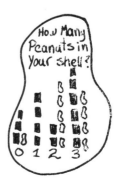

IX. Procedure—Day One

1. Peanut Background—Read and discuss information about the goober pea (what it is, where it grows, its parts, etc.)
2. Ask "Which way do you like your goober peas?" Discuss the different textures and forms in which it appears in food.
3. Pass out one brown and one yellow square of paper to each child.
4. Pass out a peanut to each child.
5. Ask the children to estimate how many peanuts they think they have in their peanut shell. Have them write their estimate in the yellow square.
6. The children will come up and record their estimate on the graph in the appropriate column.
7. Discuss the graph. (How many more...?, How many less _____ than _____?, etc.)
8. The students will open their shell, count the peanuts, and record the actual number on the peanut shaped brown paper.
9. Record the actual number next to the estimates, in the appropriate columns.
10. Discuss the graph. You may have the chance to count by 2's since you will have a nut and square together at times.
11. Eat the peanuts.

VIII. Advanced Preparation—Day Two

1. Have celery cleaned and cut.
2. Place peanuts in small bags for each group.
3. The pattern strips should be cut and the peanut pattern sheets should be copied.

IX. Procedure—Day Two

1. Give the small bag of peanuts and a measuring cup to each group (size of the cup depending on the number of groups).
2. Each group will fill up their measuring cup with shelled peanuts.
3. Discuss the recipe. (see *VI. Background Information #4*) Make the peanut butter according to the recipe.
4. Give each child a piece of celery and spread the peanut butter on it. Place peanuts or raisins on the peanut butter if you wish.
5. Eat and enjoy!
6. Pass out the copied peanut sheets and strips you have prepared for patterns. Discuss various positions the peanuts may be placed in order to create a peanut pattern.

7. Have children make their pattern strips.
8. You may want to display the strips on a chart or assemble them with a binder ring so the children can see each other's patterns.

X. Discussion

1. What happened when we put the peanuts in the blender and turned the blender on?
2. What was the most common number of peanuts in one shell?

XI. Extensions

1. How many paper clips will balance one peanut?
2. Using peanuts, how long is your desk?
3. How many peanuts will balance a block? A box of crayons?
4. Estimate how many peanuts are in a 2 lb. bag.
5. If the whole peanut weighs _____ paper clips, how many will just the meat weigh?

XII. Curriculum Coordinates

Language Arts

1. "If I were a peanut what would I be used for?" Tell me orally or written.
2. Write a recipe for peanut soup.
3. Put peanut growth pictures or sentences into sequential order.
4. Write Jimmy Carter a letter.

Art

1. Make animals or pictures out of the peanut shells.

Music

1. Learn the song "Goober Peas."

Physical Education

1. Play relay races using peanuts.
2. Play a peanut toss. How far can you and your partner toss a peanut to each other before dropping it?
3. Roll or blow a peanut as far as you can in 3 minutes.

Social Studies

1. Read about George Washington Carver and his uses for the peanut. Draw a picture of an invention you would invent.
2. Read about James Carter, President, a peanut farmer.

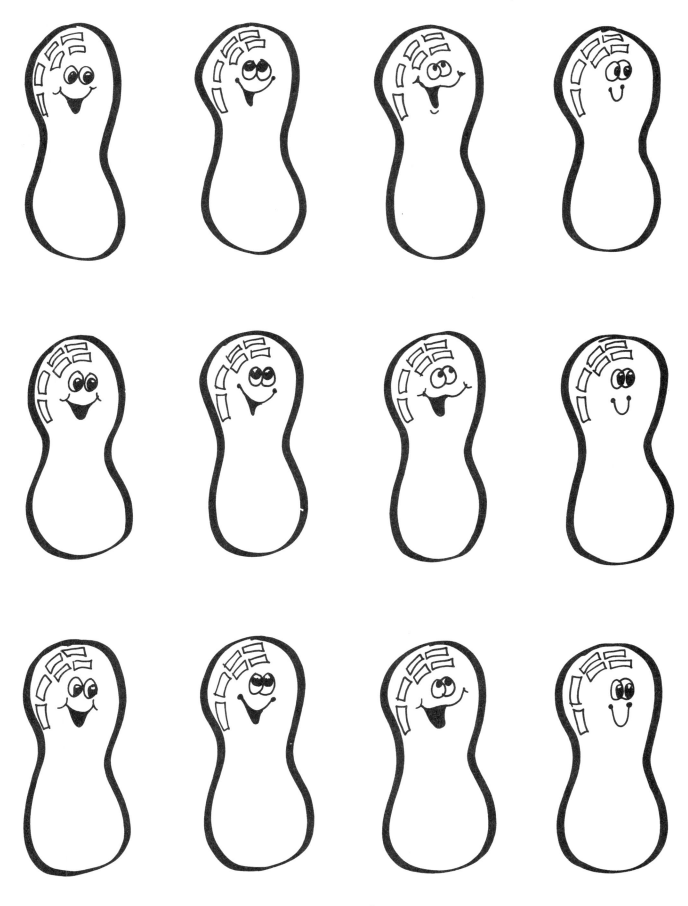

24

Mighty Mittens

I. Topic Area
Seasons-Winter

II. Introductory Statement
Students will learn about appropriate winter clothing.

III. Key Question
What kinds of clothing do you wear in winter?

IV. Math Skills
a. Attributes
b. Counting
c. Graphing
d. Interpreting data
e. Recording data
f. Sorting

Science Processes
a. Observing and classifying
b. Gathering and recording data
c. Interpreting data

V. Materials
- multi-colored construction paper (enough for four 9 × 12 sheets per child)
- multi-colored yarn (cut in 2 ft. lengths, enough for one per child)
- crayons
- scissors
- glue
- stapler
- large tagboard mitten patterns (see Pattern Sheet #1—teacher should cut out enough for one for every two children, and they may share)
- small construction paper mittens (see small mitten pattern on following page #2; teacher should cut out one for every child, corresponding to what color their mittens are)
- manila construction paper for graph
- tagboard for large mitten patterns

VI. Background Information
1. Do this activity during the winter months.

VII. Management
1. Making the mittens may take 30 minutes.
2. Graphing may take 30 minutes.
3. Let the children have a break or a recess between making the mittens and graphing.

VIII. Advanced Preparation
1. Have these materials out and ready to be used:
   multi-colored construction paper
   multi-colored yarn
   crayons
   scissors
   glue
   large tagboard mitten patterns
2. Have these materials out and ready for the graph:
   small construction paper mittens
   construction paper graph

IX. Procedure
1. Discuss: "What kinds of clothing do you wear in winter?"
2. Let the children "show and tell" about some of the winter clothing they have worn to school that day.
3. Tell the children that they are going to make one kind of winter clothing—mittens.
4. Show the children how to make the mittens:
   a. Students will choose four sheets of construction paper of the same color.
   b. They will trace the large tagboard mitten pattern on each piece of construction paper.
   c. Students will cut out the mittens.
   d. Students will glue the first two mittens together, matching edges. Then they will glue the last two mittens together, matching the edges. (They should now have a pair of mittens.)
   e. The teacher will attach a string of yarn to the bottom of the mittens with a stapler:

f. Students will color designs on the mittens.

5. After the children are done, have everyone sit on the floor with their mittens.

6. Have all the children group themselves according to their color of mittens in different areas of the room.

   Example: All the children with blue mittens, sit in one corner.
   All the children with red mittens, sit in another corner.
   Etc.

   Continue this procedure until all the children are "sorted" into groups according to their color of mittens.

7. Next, have the children make a "real graph."
   a. Have the children with blue mittens form a line, holding their mittens.
   b. Next to them, have the children with red mittens form a line, etc., until all the children are in the form of a "real graph."

   c. Discuss the real graph.
      Example: "How many children made red mittens?"
      "How many children made blue mittens?"
      "What color has the most mittens?"
      "What color has the least mittens?"

8. Introduce the "picture graph" to the children.
   a. Give each child a small construction paper mitten the color of the large mittens he/she has already made.

   b. Have each child glue their small mitten on the graph next to the appropriate color word:
   Sample Graph:

   c. Discuss the picture graph.
      Example: "How many blue and red mittens are there all together?"
      "How many children made zero mittens?"
      "How many more green mittens are there than red mittens?"

X. Discussion
   1. What's the difference between mittens and gloves?
   2. What are real mittens made of?

XII. Curriculum Coordinates
   Language Arts
   1. Recite "Three Little Kittens Lost Their Mittens"
   Music
   1. Sing to the tune of "10 Little Indians":
      One little, two little, three little mittens,
      Four little, five little, six little mittens,
      Seven little, eight little, nine little mittens,
      Ten little mittens on our hands.

large mitten pattern
for tracing 2

GLIDE INTO WINTER

27

© 1987 AIMS Education Foundation

small mitten pattern
for graphing

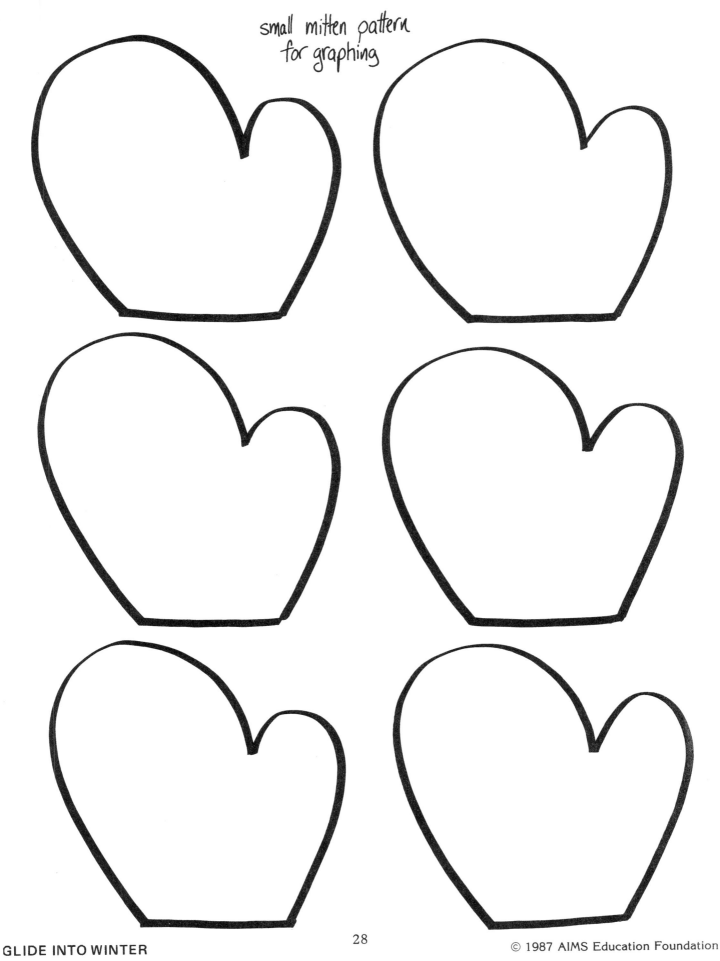

28

Electric Breakfast I.

I. Topic Area
Static Electricity

II. Introductory Statement
Students will learn that friction causes static electricity.

III. Key Question
How can you move the banana without touching it?

IV. Math Skills
a. Graphing
  1. Recording data
  2. Interpreting data
  3. Whole number computation
  4. Counting
b. Comparing
c. Predicting
d. Observing
e. Controlling variables

Science Processes
a. Observing
b. Classifying
c. Gathering and recording data
d. Interpreting data
e. Applying and generalizing
f. Controlling variables

V. Materials
- 1 blown up balloon for each child will work the best
- a piece of wool or fur
- 1 banana hanging by a string from a chart stand or a stationary rod
- butcher paper for graph approximately 18" × 48"
- 3" × 3" white squares (one for each child)
- A list of objects found in the room (i.e. sweater, jeans, hair, desk, chair, window, bags, shoe, rug, sidewalk, grass, jacket, etc.) You need to have one object for each child. The child draws the object on their 3 × 3 square.

VI. Background Information
1. Static electricity activities always work best when humidity is low and the air is dry.
2. Friction causes static electricity. When 2 different materials—especially nonmetals—are rubbed together they produce electrical charges that attract light objects. This kind of electricity does not move and is called static or stationary electricity.
3. It saves time to blow up the balloons with an air pump.

VII. Management
1. Tie the string to the banana and attach the string to something so the banana can rotate easily, such as, chart stand or a springrod in a doorway.
2. This activity can be done in one day as a whole class in about 45 minutes.
3. Have the balloons blown up ahead of time, using each balloon once.

VIII. Advanced Preparation
1. Make a list on the chalkboard of common objects found in the room (See *V. Materials* for example).
2. Prepare the graph.

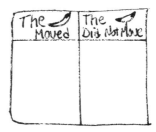

3. Cut one 3" × 3" white square for each child.
4. Suspend the banana so that it can rotate easily.

IX. Procedure

1. Have the children read the names of the objects from the board.
2. Assign one object to each child and have him draw it on the 3″ × 3″ piece of paper.
3. Put the graph on the floor.
4. Bring out the suspended banana.
5. Briskly rub the balloon several times with a piece of wool.
6. Hold the balloon beside the banana, near one end. The balloon should attract the banana and make it start to rotate. Keep the balloon near the end, but not letting it touch. Then try to reverse the rotation of the banana by holding the balloon at the other end.
7. Have the children predict if the object on their paper will move the banana and record these predictions on the graph on the floor (just place the picture on the graph, don't glue them down yet). Discuss the graph.
8. Choose 2 children. Give each of them a balloon. They find the real object that their picture represents and rub the balloon several times over the object.
9. Have each child put the balloon near the banana to see whether or not it will cause it to rotate. Leave the picture where it is on the graph or move it to the appropriate column, glueing it down this time.
10. Have the two children pass the balloon to a friend and repeat steps 8 and 9 until every child has had a turn.
11. Discuss the graph again.
12. Hang the graph up somewhere in the room.

X. Discussion

1. What objects other than the balloon could we use to create static electricity and rotate the banana?
2. What object, other than the banana could we try to move using static electricity.

XI. Extensions

What other objects could be used to produce static electricity in the balloon and cause the banana to rotate? In your free time find an object in the room we have not tried yet. Draw a picture of that object. Get the balloon and repeat what we did as a whole class. Record your findings on the new graph.

XII. Curriculum Coordinates

Language Arts

1. If your body was full of static electricity, what would you want to always stick to you? Tell me, orally or written.
2. What would you be sure to stay away from if you were full of static electricity? Tell me, orally or written.
3. If you could design a machine that would make enough static electricity to move anything, what would you move? Design that machine.

Physical Education

1. Have the children take off their shoes and shuffle across the floor. Walk around the room to touch things and make shocks.

Science

1. Take a blown up balloon and rub against your clothes. Hold the balloon over a pile of salt. Watch what happens! Rub the balloon again. Hold the balloon over a pile of sugar. Watch what happens!

Electric Breakfast I

1. Make a list on the chalkboard of objects found in the room.

sweater	desk	rug	chair
jeans	window	sidewalk	pants
hair	bags	grass	dress
jacket	shoe	door	gloves

2. Give each child a 3"x3" white piece of construction paper. Have them draw an object from the list.

3. Prepare the graph

4. Suspend the banana from the doorframe or chart stand so it hangs freely.

Place graph on floor

butcher paper

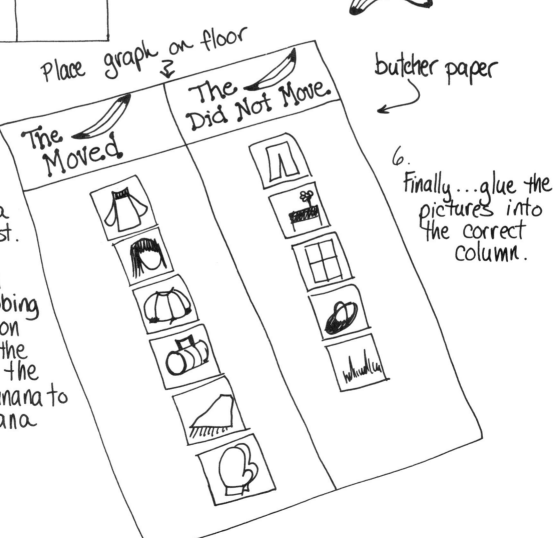

5. Have students place their drawings as a prediction first.

Then test each object by rubbing with a balloon and holding the balloon near the end of the banana to see if the banana moves.

6. Finally... glue the pictures into the correct column.

Electric Breakfast II.

I. Topic Area
Static Electricity

II. Introductory Statement
The students will learn that friction causes static electricity.

III. Key Question
How can we get the cereal to stay on the plastic wrap when the cup is rightside-up?

IV. Math Skills
a. Graphing
  1. Recording data
  2. Interpreting data
  3. Counting
  4. Whole number computation
b. Predicting
c. Observing

Science Processes
a. Observing and classifying
b. Gathering and recording data
c. Interpreting data

V. Materials
- Clear plastic cups—1 for each child
- Rice Krispies
- One square of plastic wrap to cover the top of each cup
- One rubberband for each cup
- Graph and markers
- Strips of dark construction paper, 1½" × 9", one for each child for pattern strips
- Paper plates

VI. Background Information
1. You may want to see some static electricity in "Electric Breakfast I."
2. Static electricity activities always work best when humidity is low and the air is dry.
3. Friction causes static electricity. When two different materials—especially nonmetals—are rubbed together they produce electrical charges that attract light objects. This kind of electricity does not move and is called static or stationary electricity.

VII. Management
1. This activity works well in conjunction with "Electric Breakfast I."
2. This activity can be done as a total class, teacher-directed activity, however students should be sitting in groups of 7-8 children.
3. This activity will take about 30 minutes depending on the extent of discussion you feel is appropriate.

VIII. Advanced Preparation
1. Have the plastic wrap squares cut.
2. Prepare the graph. Cut 1" squares to mark predictions.

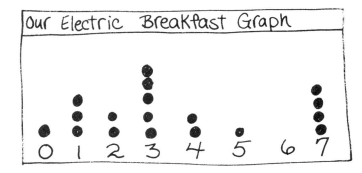

IX. Procedure
1. To each group hand out the following to make the cereal cups;
   a. Cups
   b. One plate to each group filled with cereal.
   c. Ask the children to put 7 pieces in their cup.
   d. Pass out the plastic wrap squares and place over the top of the cup.
   e. Help the children put the rubberband around the cup.
2. If you have not done "Electric Breakfast I" explain how rubbing the plastic on different objects will cause static electricity. If you have done "Electric Breakfast I" ask for ideas on how we can get the cereal to stick.

3. Display the graph. Ask the children to predict, "How many pieces of cereal you can get to stick to the top of the cup on the plastic wrap?"
4. Record the predictions and discuss the graph.
5. Review the "Electric Breakfast I" lesson or some activity to get the children to discover that friction causes static electricity.
6. Let the children explore and try to get as many pieces as possible to stick. Helpful Hint: Rubbing the cup and plastic wrap on their hair gets good results quickly.
7. After several minutes stop the activity. Check and discuss which surfaces produced the most static electricity.

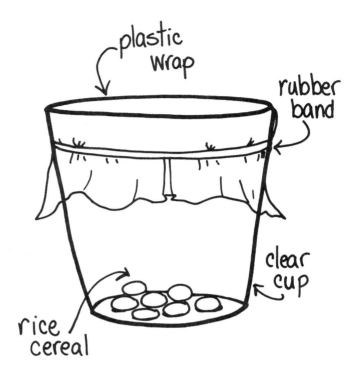

X. **Discussion**
1. What objects worked well when rubbed? Which didn't?
2. What else besides Rice Krispies might stick to the plastic?

XI. **Extensions**
1. Using the dark paper that is cut into strips for patterns, glue the cereal down in different positions to make a pattern.
2. How many pieces of cereal will balance a paper clip?
3. How many pieces of cereal will cover a 1" square (measuring area)
4. Rub a balloon on your hair or sweater and hold it over a pile of salt. Watch what happens!
5. Rub the balloon again and hold it over a pile of sugar. Watch what happens!
6. Game. "I'm rubbing you with a *sweater.* Are you jumping?"
7. Pass out a little handful of cereal. Count by ones, twos, etc.

XII. **Curriculum Coordinates**
Language Arts
1. Design and name a new kind of cereal and its box.
2. Put pictures or sentences into sequence about how we made the cereal cups.
3. Write or draw the directions for making a bowl of cereal for breakfast.
Cooking
1. Make Rice Krispies Squares.
Art
1. Make a picture with several different types of cereal.

clear cup

plastic wrap

rubber band

rice cereal

1.

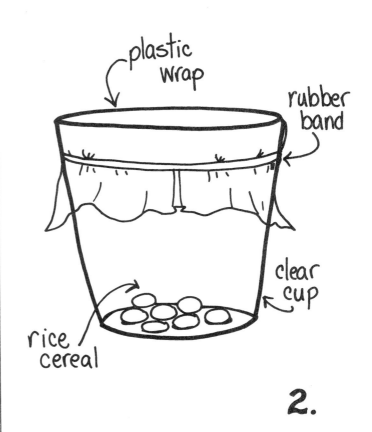

plastic wrap

rubber band

clear cup

rice cereal

2.

3.

4.

Valentine Candy Count

I. Topic Area
Valentine candy (seasonal foods)

II. Introductory Statement
Students will discover what color valentine candy is found more often than any other in a standard bag of valentine candy.

III. Key Question
What color of valentine candy do you think we will find more often than any of the other colors?

IV. Math Skills
a. Predicting
b. Sorting
c. Classifying
d. Graphing
   1. Counting
   2. Equations

Science Processes
a. Observing and classifying
b. Gathering and recording data
c. Interpreting data
d. Applying and generalizing

V. Materials
- 12 oz. bag of "Tiny Conversation Hearts"
- glass decanter (large enough to hold all of the hearts)
- styrofoam cups (1 cup for every 4-6 students)
- pencils
- crayons (1 crayon for each color of valentine candy)
- Prediction Graph
- Final Results Graph
- valentine name tags (with students' names written on them)
- sorting/classifying sheets
- student recording sheet (1 for each group of 4-6 students)

VI. Background Information
A glue stick works well when attaching the initial predictions to the prediction graph.

VII. Management
1. This activity takes approximately 60 minutes.
2. Students work in a total class situation when predicting and graphing their data.
3. Students work in groups of 4-6 when classifying and sorting.

VIII. Advanced Preparation
1. Prepare individual name tag valentines with students' names written on them.
2. Prepare the prediction graph.
3. Place the student name valentines and the glue stick near the prediction graph.
4. Prepare the final results graph. (place the crayons nearby)
5. Place both graphs in an area where the children will be able to see them, as well as reach them.
6. Prepare copies of the student recording sheet. (1/group of 4-6 students)
7. Prepare copies of the sorting/classifying sheets. (1/group of 4-6 students)
8. Place all of the valentine candy into the glass decanter so that the children can make their initial predictions.
9. As soon as the initial predictions have been made and recorded, divide the candy and place it into the styrofoam cups. (each group of 4-6 students will get a cup of candy)

IX. Procedure
1. Students predict which color candy they think will be found most frequently by placing their name valentines on the appropriate color valentine on the prediction graph. (total class)
2. Students sort and classify a "cup-full" of valentine candy according to color on their sorting/classifying sheets. (small groups)
3. Students record their color counts on the student recording sheet. (one member of the group records the counts while the rest of the group counts)
4. Students graph their results on the final results graph. (graph one color at a time—one student from each group graphs one color—all students will have a turn to graph a color)

X. Discussion

1. How many __(color)__ valentines did we find? How many...?
2. What color did we find more of than any other?
3. Did the prediction that you made turn out to be true?
4. What if we bought a new bag of candy—would we find the same number of each color of candy? Why? Why not?

XI. Extensions

1. Repeat the procedure using a new bag of candy and compare the results.
2. Count the candy.

XII. Curriculum Coordinates

Language Arts

1. *Happy/Sad Valentines*
   —children make the Happy/Sad Valentines
   —children take turns saying, "I am happy (show happy valentine) when..." (repeat for the sad valentine
   —as a variation, the teacher says something that will elicit a happy/sad response and the children show the appropriate valentine and say, "*(what the teacher said)* makes me happy/sad." (it is sometimes helpful to write what the teacher says on the chalkboard in order to help the children remember.

Art

1. Valentine flowers.

Valentine Candy Count Graphs

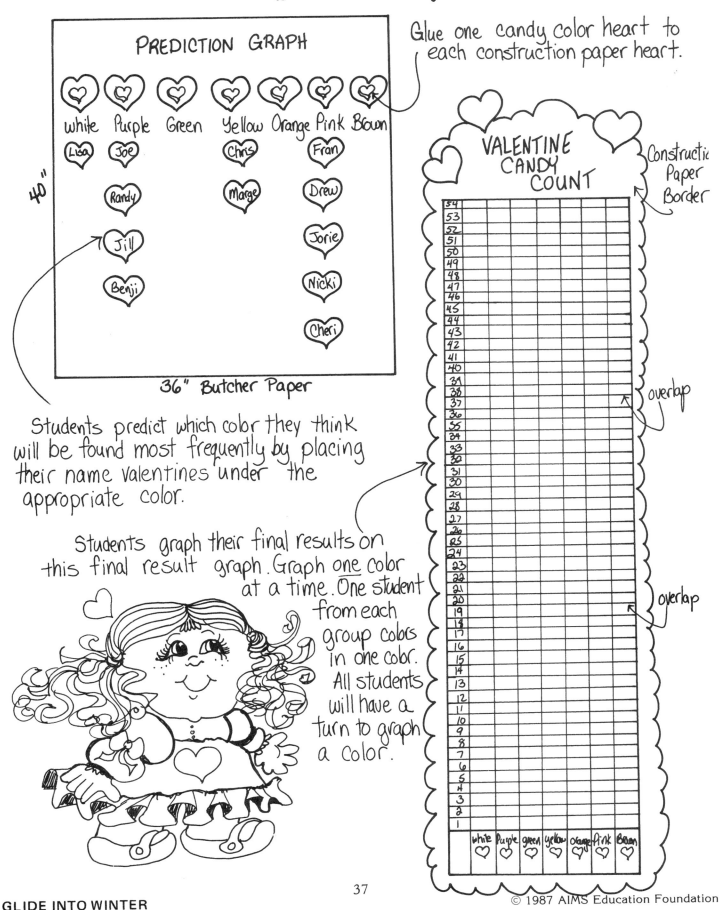

PREDICTION GRAPH

white	Purple	Green	Yellow	Orange	Pink	Brown
Lisa	Joe		Chris		Fran	
Randy			Marge		Drew	
Jill					Jorie	
Benji					Nicki	
					Cheri	

40"

36" Butcher Paper

Glue one candy color heart to each construction paper heart.

VALENTINE CANDY COUNT

Constructic Paper Border

overlap

overlap

Students predict which color they think will be found most frequently by placing their name valentines under the appropriate color.

Students graph their final results on this final result graph. Graph one color at a time. One student from each group colors in one color. All students will have a turn to graph a color.

	white ♥	Purple ♥	green ♥	yellow ♥	orange ♥	Pink ♥	Brown ♥

54 53 52 51 50 49 48 47 46 45 44 43 42 41 40 39 38 37 36 35 34 33 32 31 30 29 28 27 26 25 24 23 22 21 20 19 18 17 16 15 14 13 12 11 10 9 8 7 6 5 4 3 2 1

GLIDE INTO WINTER

Valentine Candy Count

Name_____

How many ♡'s
did you find?

white ♡'s _____
purple ♡'s _____
green ♡'s _____
yellow ♡'s _____
orange ♡'s _____
pink ♡'s _____
brown ♡'s _____

GLIDE INTO WINTER

Please put me where I belong

Sorting Sheet

GLIDE INTO WINTER

NUMBER OF HEARTS	white ♡	purple ♡	green ♡	yellow ♡	orange ♡	pink ♡	brown ♡

GLIDE INTO WINTER

40

GLIDE INTO WINTER

You Are All Heart

I. Topic Area
Human Body: The Heart

II. Introductory Statement
Students will discover what causes differences in the rate of the heartbeat.

III. Key Question
"How many times does your heart beat during recess time; how many times does your heart beat during rest time?"

IV. Math Skills
a. Counting
b. Timing
c. Graphing
  1. Counting
  2. Comparing
  3. Interpreting data
  4. One-to-correspondence
  5. Recording data
  6. Set theory
  7. Whole number computation

Science Processes
a. Measuring
b. Controlling variables
c. Gathering and recording data
d. Interpreting data
e. Applying and generalizing

V. Materials
- stethoscope (if not available, your finger may be used to lightly tough the child's wrist)
- stop watch (or a clock with a seconds hand)
- two large pieces of tagboard, for graphs, and "heart" markers made out of pink or red construction paper, for graphing

VI. Background Information
1. The teacher should be familiar with using the stethoscope.
2. The teacher should know where to find a child's pulse. The easiest place to feel the pulse is either on the wrist or on either side of the throat.
3. Some children's heartbeats are very light and hard to detect. Some are very pronounced and easy to detect.

VII. Management
1. This activity may take twenty minutes.
2. To save time, time each child's heartbeat for ten seconds and multiply by six to get a reading for one minute. Or, if your children cannot recognize larger numbers, simply time each child's heartbeat for ten seconds only. The numbers will then remain smaller.

VIII. Advanced Preparation
1. Have out and ready to use: a stethoscope and a stop watch.

IX. Procedure
1. Ask the children to show you where their hearts are located.
2. Let them listen to their heartbeats with a stethoscope or just feel their heartbeat with their hand.
3. Show the children other places on their bodies where they can feel their hearts "beat" (wrist, sides of the throat).
4. Ask the children if they think their hearts beat faster during recess time or during rest time.
5. One at a time, have the students listen to and count their heartbeats in a ten second period during recess time. (Teacher may have to assist.) Multiply by six to get a one minute reading.
6. Record on a heart graph.

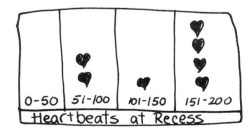

© 1987 AIMS Education Foundation

7. Repeat the same procedure during rest time and record the results.

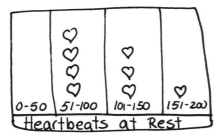

Put each child's name and number of heartbeats on each heart

X. Discussion
1. When does the heart beat faster...during recess time or during rest time?
2. Why does the heart beat slower during rest time?
3. What is the heart's job?

XI. Extensions
1. Take your heartbeat while: jumping, sitting, walking.
2. Examine a real heart from a cow, chicken, turkey, etc.

XII. Curriculum Coordinates
Lanauage Arts
1. Recite "The Queen of Hearts" nursery rhyme.
Art
1. Make a man out of heart shapes.

Music
1. Listen to: "I Left My Heart in San Francisco"
2. Sing "Will You Be a Friend of Mine?" Sing to the tune of "Mary Had A Little Lamb." (Have a child give a paper heart to a friend while singing.)
> Will you be a friend of mine, friend of mine, friend of mine.
> Will you be a friend of mine and take this heart of mine!

Physical Education
1. Do activities to make your heart beat faster: running, skipping, relay races, etc.
2. Do activities to make your heart beat slower: relax like a limp rag doll, sit very still, etc.

patterns
for
graph

GLIDE INTO WINTER

All Aboard the Chow Express

I. Topic Area
Nutrition

II. Introductory Statement
Students will learn the Four Basic Food Groups and what foods are contained in each.

III. Key Question
What kinds of different groups can we separate foods into?

IV. Math Skills
a. Set theory
b. Sorting
c. Observing
d. Logical thinking
e. Interpreting data
f. Counting
g. Generalizing
h. Attributes

Science Processes
a. Observing and classifying
b. Controlling variable
c. Gathering and recording data
d. Interpreting data
e. Applying and generalizing

V. Materials
- Assorted magazine or hand-drawn pictures of foods from the four food groups, mounted on tagboard and laminated
- 4 large manila envelopes, each labeled with 1 of the Basic Food Groups
- For food train (session two)
  4 slices of carrots per child
  1 piece of celery per child (⅓ of stalk)
  2 toothpicks per child
  Peanut butter, cottage cheese, or spreadable cheese to stuff inside of celery
  Alfalfa sprouts

VI. Background Information
1. The tune to be used for the "Food Groups Journey" is the 1930's song "Sentimental Journey." If this is not familiar to the teacher, a substitute tune will need to be selected prior to the session one activities.

The Food Groups Journey
I'm going to take you on the Food Groups Journey
In a food train built by you.
Come on along, on the Food Groups Journey,
And see what good foods can do for you.

2. The students should have prior experience with grouping foods according to the Basic Foods Groups. This is an excellent culminating activity for a unit on nutrition.

VII. Management
1. This activity works best when divided into two sessions:
   a. Session One will take approximately 30-40 minutes when conducted in a whole class setting. During this time period, there will be discussions about the Four Basic Food Groups, and the "Food Groups Journey" will take place.
   b. Session Two will take approximately 20-30 minutes and is most easily conducted in small groups of 4-5 students. In this session, the students will construct and eat their food trains according to the teacher's specifications.

VIII. Advanced Preparation
For Session One:
1. Cut out, mount on tagboard, and laminate magazine pictures of various foods. Be sure to include a variety of foods from each group.
2. Prepare four manila envelopes with one of the four food groups drawn or written on the outside of the envelope. Place the envelopes in four different locations of the room, accessible to small groups of children.

For Session Two:
1. Cut and clean vegetable for food trains (see *Materials* for specified quantities).

IX. Procedure

Session One:

1. The teacher asks the key question while showing food cards, "How might we separate these foods into different groups?" When the Basic Food Groups are mentioned, name them and give examples.

2. The teacher tells the children that they are going to take a food groups journey. In order to get on and off the food train, they must be able to tell the names of foods and the basic food groups they belong to. Show the children the cards and have the entire class place them into the four food groups.

3. Teach the children the song, "Food Groups Journey."

4. Pass out one food card per student. This will be their train ticket.

5. Have the class line up in one long line behind the teacher. Travel around the room, singing the "Food Groups Journey." As the train approaches a train stop (envelope with one of the food groups on it), announce to the train passengers that you will be stopping at _____ Street (Bread and Cereal, Meat and Protein, Fruit and Vegetable, or Dairy Group). Any child holding a ticket with a picture of a food contained in that group may get off at the stop by naming the food on their ticket and the food group it belongs to. The students will step off the train and place their ticket in the manila envelope. They will remain at the stop until re-boarding time. Have the passengers remaining on the train count the number of children who disembarked. The children who left the train will count the number of children still remaining on the train. Repeat this procedure, stopping at each of the departure points, until the train is empty.

6. Continue traveling around the room, re-filling the train in the same manner as it was emptied; have each child pull a ticket from their group's envelope, name the food on it and the food group it belongs to. You might want to exchange the group's envelopes so the children can experience working with two different food groups. When the train is once again full, have the students return to their seats for discussion.

Session Two

1. Each group of 4-5 students should have the needed food ingredients in front of them. Have each child construct a food train according to the following specifications:
   a. Insert toothpicks at both ends of the celery to form the axles for the wheels of the train.
   b. Place a slice of carrot at the end of each toothpick to form the four wheels.
   c. Stuff the celery with the desired filling, and top with alfalfa sprouts.
   d. Eat.

X. Discussion

1. Did we name all the foods in each food group during our journey? What are some of the foods that we did not mention? What food groups do they belong to?

2. What other kinds of vegetables could we use to make our trains?

XI. Extensions

1. Have the children construct other types of transportation using vegetables of their choice.

XII. Curriculum Coordinates

Languages Arts

1. Have each child write or dictate a story about their favorite food.

2. Invent a recipe using ingredients from each of the four food groups.

Music

1. Sing, "Simple Sal."

Art

1. Make fruit and vegetable prints. Dip sliced fruits and vegetables in tempera paint and print on construction paper.

Meat-Fish

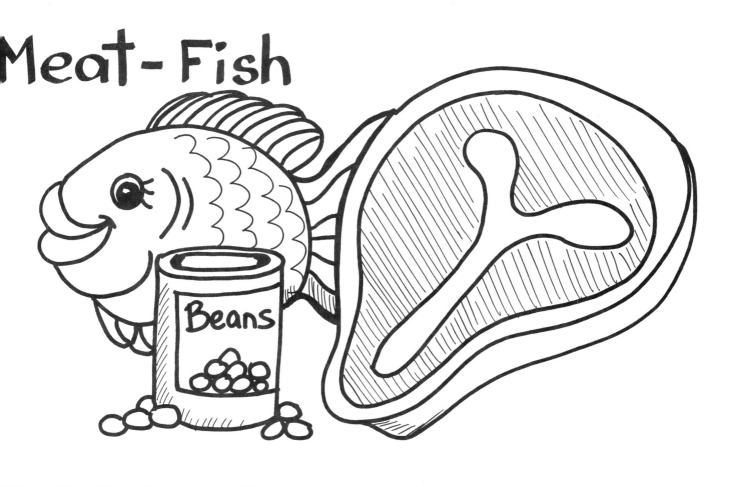

Beans

Milk Group

Milk

Yogurt

47

Fruits-Vegetables

Breads and Cereals

48

ice cream

Yogurt

ice cream

cheese

Milkshake

Milk

pancakes

Cottage Cheese

rice

Cake

tortilla

cereal

muffin

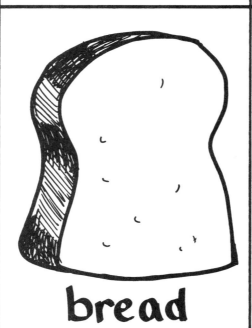

bread

spaghetti

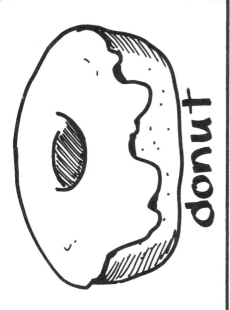

donut

ham

chicken

shrimp

bacon

sausage

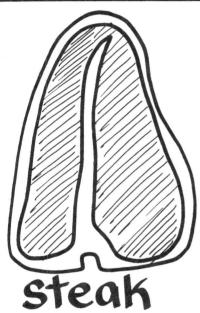
steak

fish

eggs

peanuts

hamburger
pattie

51

peanut
butter

peas

beet

onions

broccoli

carrot

celery

corn

lettuce

potato

52

Only the Nose Knows

I. Topic Area
The five senses

II. Introductory Statement
The students will learn that in many instances two or more of their senses work together to give them information.

III. Math Skills
a. Attributes
b. Counting
c. Equations
d. Formula usage
e. Fractions
f. Graphing
g. Measuring volume
h. Predicting
i. Variables

Science Processes
a. Observing and classifying
b. Measuring
c. Controlling Variables
d. Gathering and recording data
e. Interpreting data
f. Applying and generalizing

IV. Materials
- 1 package unflavored gelatin (4 envelopes per package). You will need 2 envelopes per color for a 32 pupil class.
- 12 × 8 × 2 inch pans
- 4 tablespoons sugar
- measuring cups and spoons
- boiling water
- desired food coloring
- teacher made prediction chart and 2 construction paper squares of each color per child
- wax paper

V. Background Information
1. Students will need to have previous experiences and knowledge involving the 5 senses and how they work.

VII. Management
1. The activity needs to be conducted over a two day period.
   a. *Day 1:* The gelatin is made in small groups with direct teacher supervision, then put in the refrigerator overnight to gel. The teacher will need to have put the food coloring in the water before the children meet in groups (this can be referred to as the secret flavoring.)
   b. *Day 2:* The whole class meets to sample the gelatin and make predictions.
2. *Gelatin Recipe*
   1 envelope unflavored gelatin
   2 tablespoons sugar
   2 cups boiling water
   food coloring

VIII. Teacher Preparation
1. Mix the food coloring and boiling water in a pitcher or jar.
2. Prepare the class graphs, one per color, allowing space for 4-5 flavor guesses.

3. Cut colored construction paper into squares (2 per color per child).

IX. Procedure
Day 1
1. The students will meet in small groups of 6-8 children and prepare the gelatin.
Day 2
1. The students will look at the gelatin and brainstorm possible flavors solely by the use of this sense. The teacher will write all possibilities on the chalkboard.
2. Each student will choose their flavor prediction and place their corresponding marker on the graph.
3. The students will smell the gelatin and brainstorm possible flavors solely by the use of this sense. The teacher will write all possibilities on the chalkboard.
4. Each student will choose their flavor prediction and place their corresponding marker on the graph.
5. The students will taste the gelatin and brainstorm possible flavors solely by use of this sense. The teacher will write all possibilities on the chalkboard.
6. Each student will choose their flavor prediction and place their corresponding marker on the graph.
7. Repeat for each color of gelatin.

X. Discussion
1. Review the information gathered on the graph.
2. The teacher will announce that all the predictions are incorrect. Why?
3. Discuss what role the eyes and nose play in fooling our taste buds.
4. How did your previous experiences help to fool your tongue?
5. Can you think of any other foods that taste different than they look? Do you try them, or do you allow your eyes to fool your tongue?

XI. Curriculum Coordinates
Language Arts
1. Write experience stories about:
   Our Tricky Eyes
   Foods That Taste Better Than They Look
   My Favorite Foods Are . . .
Music
1. Sing: My Favorite Things, from Sound of Music. Perform with props from song.
Art
1. Make a magazine collage of favorite things to eat.
2. Have students make individual "My Favorite Things" booklet.

My Favorite Things

a Unit about the 5 senses

Published by:
Date _____
Teacher _____
School _____

54

These are my favorite things to taste

My name is _____

This book is about a few of my favorite things.

I hope you like it.

These are my favorite things to see 🕷 .

These are my favorite things to hear 👂 .

These are my favorite things to touch.

These are my favorite things to smell.

57

Do You Have a Snoot for Fruit?

I. Topic Area
Sense of Smell

II. Introductory Statement
Students will smell three different fruits blind-folded and name the fruits.

III. Key Question
Can you name these fruits without seeing them? How could we do that?

IV. Math Skills
a. Inferring
b. Problem solving
c. Classifying
d. Predictions
e. Graphing
  1. Counting
  2. Whole number computation
  3. Recording data/ Interpreting data

Science Processes
a. Observing and classifying
b. Recording data
c. Interpreting data

V. Materials
- Apples, bananas, oranges (enough for each child to sample his/her favorite)
- Cutting board
- Knife
- Blindfold (see pattern sheet #2)
- Graph
- Small paper for each child with their name previously written

VI. Background Information
Caution the students never to place their faces over objects to smell them. Review proper method used in smelling unknown objects as a precautionary measure, in case students go home and smell objects that could be harmful. Remind the students a "gentle" sniff will do it!

VII. Management
1. This activity should take about 20 minutes.
2. It could be done as a whole group or in small groups.

VIII. Advanced Preparation
1. Prepare a small paper for each child, about 1" × 3", and write their name on each paper.
2. Graph for the children to place the paper that indicates their choice of their favorite fruit. Paper should be at least 18" × 24" and at the top place a picture or draw a picture of an apple, banana, and an orange. (Drawings of these fruits are at the end of this lesson.)

IX. Procedure
1. Show the students the apple, orange, and banana. What kinds of foods are they?
2. Could you tell the name of these fruits without seeing them? How could we do that?
3. How many of you think more of you like apples the best? How many of you think more of you like oranges the best? How many of you think more of you like bananas the best?
4. Proceed to cut the fruits yourself but have the students infer why the fruits are being cut in half rather than leaving them whole.
5. Allow each child to wear the blindfold and the teacher holds one fruit at a time near the child. The child identifies each of the three fruits. Remove the blindfold at the end of the child's turn.
6. Which of these fruits did you like the best? Give the child a sample to eat of the fruit. The student places his/her name under that fruit on the graph.

Apple	Orange	Banana
	Sara	
	Toni	
	Jimmy	David
Ed	Benji	Catricia
Flora	Michelle	Laquesta
Lorraine	Mikey	Troy
Lori	Jeri	Linda

7. When everyone has had a turn the graph is finished and you can make all the comparisons on the graph, such as whole number computation, equations, and counting.

X. Discussion
1. How can you tell the name of something without seeing it?
2. Do all foods taste good to you?
3. Can you tell me some good smells?
4. Can you tell me some bad smells?
5. Could some smells warn us of danger?

XI. Extension
1. Do the whole procedure again using different fruits, or use other foods such as peanut butter, cheese, pickles.
2. For further practice in smelling to identify use the following odors: bacon, perfume strawberries, lemons, oranges, onion, banana, peppermint, and cinnamon. Use a small container with a lid, such as a film cannister for each fragrance. Use extract flavoring for orange, lemon, banana, strawberry, peppermint, and place on a cotton ball. Use bacon bits, dried onion, and instant coffee for those odors. Students smell each container and match it to the picture on the following pages. Over a period of several days when all the children have had a turn you can graph those fragrances the students liked and did not like.

XII. Curriculum Coordinates
Language Arts
1. Make a class book about foods the students like because of the way they taste.
2. Read *Follow Your Nose* by Paul Showers.

Art
1. Have the students draw objects they like to smell and objects they do not like to smell.

Math
1. Make patterns on skewers using real fruit.

Do You Have a Snoot for Fruit?

1. Allow each child to wear the clown blindfold. Hold one fruit at a time near the child.
2. After the child identifies each of the three fruits, remove the blindfold.
3. Ask the child which of these 3 fruits did he/she like the best? Give the child a sample to eat of that fruit. Have the student place his or her name under that fruit on the graph.
4. When everyone has had a turn, the graph is finished and you can then make comparisons such as whole number computations, equations, and counting.

Apple	Orange	Banana
	Sara	
	Toni	
	Jimmy	David
Ed	Benji	Latricia
Flora	Michelle	Laquesha
Lorraine	Mikey	Troy
Lori	Jeri	Linda

EXTENSIONS: Do the entire procedure again using different fruits or other foods. On the following pages, you will find patterns for this activity. Print on tag board and color, then laminate. Have students smell the substances, then match the smells to the pictures.

peppermint

Suggested Smells:
peanut butter, cheese pickles, bacon, perfume, strawberries, lemon onion, peppermint, cinamon, bacon bits, extracts, instant coffee

60

Color brightly and use.

Clown Blindfold – Construct on heavy tag or poster board.
Color. Use a rubber band or add yarn to tie.

Cut out and mount on heavy p...

Do You Have a Snoot for Fruit?

Patterns for Graph

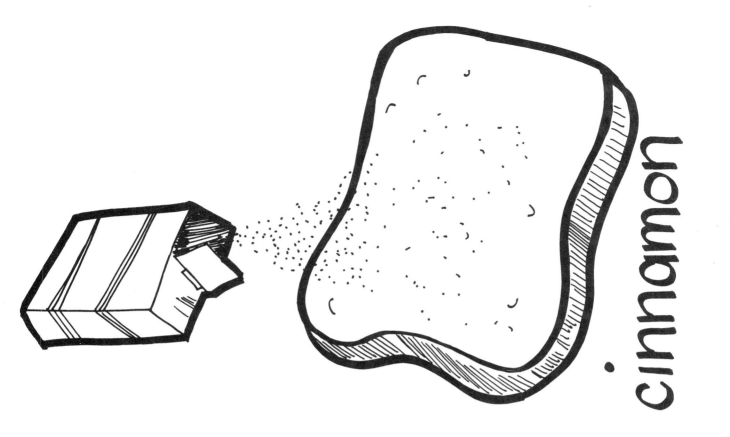

cinnamon

coffee

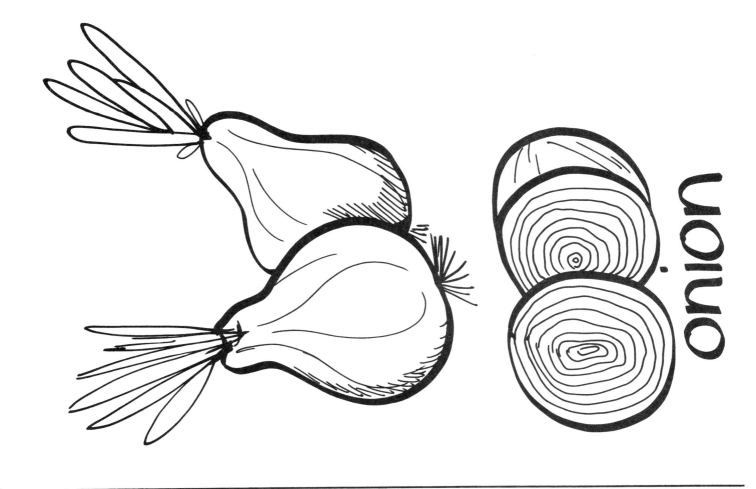

onion

perfume

orange

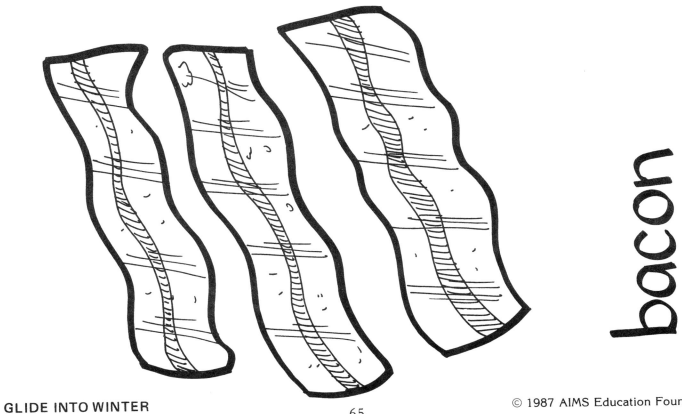

bacon

Strawberry

lemon

GLIDE INTO WINTER

peppermint

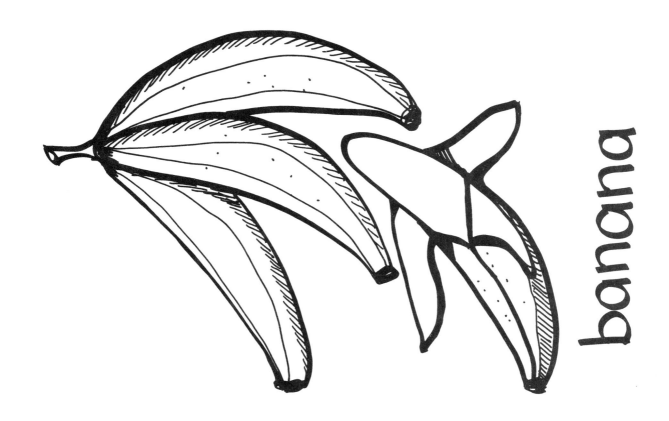

banana

GLIDE INTO WINTER

Sorda Pop

I. Topic Area
Foods

II. Introductory Statement
The students will learn what causes the bubbles in a carbonated drink.

III. Key Question
Why do some drinks "fizzle" while others do not?

IV. Math Skills
a. Applying formulas
b. Equations
c. Fractions
d. Hypothesizing
e. Measuring
f. Problem solving
g. Ratios

Science Processes
a. Observing
b. Measuring
c. Controlling variables
d. Interpreting data
e. Applying and generalizing

V. Materials
- empty soft drink bottle
- balloon
- small funnel
- baking soda
- vinegar
- styrofoam cups (1 per child)
- spoons
- fruit juice
- water

VI. Background Information
1. When soda pop mixes with vinegar or a liquid with a high acid content, carbon dioxide is formed. The gas builds up pressure in the bottle or glass and pushes out into the atmosphere, or in this case, the balloon.
2. The following recipe is for individual servings of "Sorda Pop." You will need to multiply it by the number of students in your class.

Sorda Pop
1 cup of juice
1/8 teaspoon of baking soda

Mix juice and soda in a glass. Stir well. The higher ratio of juice per baking soda, the more appealing the "pop" will be. This will decrease the amount of fizz that appears, however.

VII. Management
1. Each of the two activities will take approximately 30-40 minutes. They may be conducted in whole class or small group settings.

VIII. Advanced Preparation
1. Purchase all the necessary materials.

IX. Procedure
1. *Session One:*
   With a funnel, the teacher will carefully place 2 teaspoons of baking soda into a balloon. Pour ¼ cup vinegar into the bottle. Being careful to keep the soda in the balloon, stretch the balloon over the mouth of the bottle. Shake the baking soda out of the balloon into the vinegar. The balloon will blow up.
2. *Session Two:*
   The teacher will tell the students that they will apply what they have just learned about gases by making sorda pop. Place the juice and water into the individual cups. Add the baking soda and stir. The juice will appear to be "sorda like pop," complete with bubbles and fizz.

X. Discussion
1. What made the ballon blow up?
2. What made the bubbles in the fruit juice?
3. Can we think of other places where gases are formed?
4. What would happen if we tried other liquids for our pop? Try them.

XII. Curriculum Coordinates
Language Arts
1. Design and describe an original soda pop. Draw a picture of what the bottle would look like.
2. List and describe as many commercially produced soda pops as possible. Have the class vote for their favorites. Graph the results.

Physical Education
1. Pretend you are soda pop bubbles trying to escape a bottle.

baking
soda

Vinegar

balloon

Vinegar

1

baking
soda

Vinegar

2

baking
Soda

Vinegar
+
Baking
soda

3

gas

Vinegar
+
baking
soda

4

SORDA POP CANS FOR GRAPH OR PATTERNS

GLIDE INTO WINTER

I. Topic Area
Comparing

II. Introductory Statement
Children will compare objects and determine which is heavier.

III. Key Question
When two things seem to weigh the same, how can we decide which is heavier?

IV. Math Skills
a. Estimating
b. Observing
c. Predicting
d. Problem solving
e. Comparing
f. Graphing
 1. Counting
 2. Interpreting data

Science Processes
a. Classifying
b. Estimating
c. Interpreting data
d. Comparing
e. Gathering data

V. Materials
- Balance scale
- Two milk cartons suspended by rubber bands
- Two rulers
- Various objects to compare, such as: blocks, screws, shells, keys, parquetry blocks, jars, scissors, etc.
- Graph
- Prediction Cards (See pattern sheet page)

VII. Management
1. This activity may take approximately 15 to 20 minutes. Present to the whole clas.
2. Children can then use the materials to investigate in small groups of two or three.

VIII. Advanced Preparation
1. If you do not have a balance scale you can make your own by using two one half gallon milk cartons. Cut the cartons about three inches from the bottom. Attach one large rubber band to each carton. Hook each band to a ruler and extend the ruler over a table top. Weight the rulers down with heavy books.

Example:

2. Prepare a graph, approximately 18"×24", by dividing it in half, and labeling each half "heavier" and "lighter."

Example:

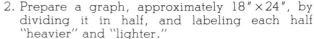

3. Prepare prediction cards by duplicating the pattern sheet and make one for each child in the group.

4. For reusable cards, make copies of the pattern sheet and cut them in half. Paste "heavier" on one side of 6"×9" construction paper or tagboard. Paste "lighter" on another 6"×9" paper. Laminate cards or cover them with clear contact.

Example:

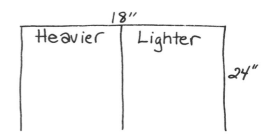

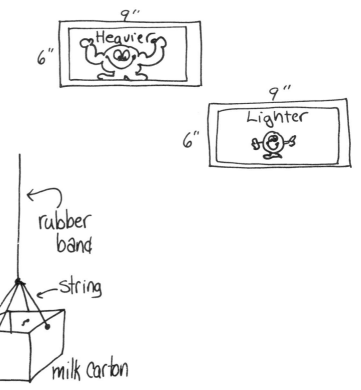

IX. Procedure

1. Discuss the meaning of heavier and lighter.

2. Give each child the heavier/lighter prediction cards. Practice using the cards so the children can tell which card shows "heavier" and which card shows "lighter."

3. Choose two objects, such as two small blocks, and discuss the size, shape, and weight of the blocks. Have the children predict with their prediction cards which block is heavier and which is lighter.

4. Have a child place a block in each carton or each side of the scale. The children tell which block was heavier.

5. The child removes the blocks from the scale and places the blocks on the appropriate sides of the graph.

6. Repeat the above procedure with all the other objects.

X. Discussion

1. When all the children have had an opportunity to explore comparing the objects discuss with the children what they have found.

2. If you find some things that seem to be the same size is it possible to arrange them in order by feeling? How can you check if you are right?

3. Do heavier things fall to the ground more quickly than lighter things? How can you find out?

XI. Extension

1. Try Bell Bags. These are the same as bean bags, except they contain bells. The bell bags are approximately 4" square. Bag one has one bell inside, bag two has two bells inside, etc. The number of bells in each bag is written on the outside of the bag. Compare two bell bags, number side down. Children guess which bag has more bells inside by feeling the weight of the bags in each hand. When they have guessed turn the bags over and see if they are correct. (The bag with more bells is a larger number.)

XII. Curriculum Coordinates

Language Arts

1. Make class books of heavy things and light things. Children draw an object that is heavy and dictate their story. These pictures go in a "heavy" book. Do the same thing for a "light" book. This would be a good beginning for opposites.

Music

1. Use the Hap Palmer record, Vol. II. "Elephant Walk." Pretend to be elephants.

Lighter

Heavier

The AIMS Program

AIMS is the acronym for "**A**ctivities **I**ntegrating **M**athematics and **S**cience." Such integration enriches learning and makes it meaningful and holistic. AIMS began as a project of Fresno Pacific University to integrate the study of mathematics and science in grades K-9, but has since expanded to include language arts, social studies, and other disciplines.

AIMS is a continuing program of the non-profit AIMS Education Foundation. It had its inception in a National Science Foundation funded program whose purpose was to explore the effectiveness of integrating mathematics and science. The project directors in cooperation with 80 elementary classroom teachers devoted two years to a thorough field-testing of the results and implications of integration.

The approach met with such positive results that the decision was made to launch a program to create instructional materials incorporating this concept. Despite the fact that thoughtful educators have long recommended an integrative approach, very little appropriate material was available in 1981 when the project began. A series of writing projects have ensued and today the AIMS Education Foundation is committed to continue the creation of new integrated activities on a permanent basis.

The AIMS program is funded through the sale of this developing series of books and proceeds from the Foundation's endowment. All net income from program and products flows into a trust fund administered by the AIMS Education Foundation. Use of these funds is restricted to support of research, development, and publication of new materials. Writers donate all their rights to the Foundation to support its on-going program. No royalties are paid to the writers.

The rationale for integration lies in the fact that science, mathematics, language arts, social studies, etc., are integrally interwoven in the real world from which it follows that they should be similarly treated in the classroom where we are preparing students to live in that world. Teachers who use the AIMS program give enthusiastic endorsement to the effectiveness of this approach.

Science encompasses the art of questioning, investigating, hypothesizing, discovering, and communicating. Mathematics is a language that provides clarity, objectivity, and understanding. The language arts provide us powerful tools of communication. Many of the major contemporary societal issues stem from advancements in science and must be studied in the context of the social sciences. Therefore, it is timely that all of us take seriously a more holistic mode of educating our students. This goal motivates all who are associated with the AIMS Program. We invite you to join us in this effort.

Meaningful integration of knowledge is a major recommendation coming from the nation's professional science and mathematics associations. The American Association for the Advancement of Science in *Science for All Americans* strongly recommends the integration of mathematics, science, and technology. The National Council of Teachers of Mathematics places strong emphasis on applications of mathematics such as are found in science investigations. AIMS is fully aligned with these recommendations.

Extensive field testing of AIMS investigations confirms these beneficial results.

1. Mathematics becomes more meaningful, hence more useful, when it is applied to situations that interest students.
2. The extent to which science is studied and understood is increased, with a significant economy of time, when mathematics and science are integrated.
3. There is improved quality of learning and retention, supporting the thesis that learning which is meaningful and relevant is more effective.
4. Motivation and involvement are increased dramatically as students investigate real-world situations and participate actively in the process. We invite you to become part of this classroom teacher movement by using an integrated approach to learning and sharing any suggestions you may have. The AIMS Program welcomes you!

AIMS Education Foundation Programs

A Day with AIMS®

Intensive one-day workshops are offered to introduce educators to the philosophy and rationale of AIMS. Participants will discuss the methodology of AIMS and the strategies by which AIMS principles may be incorporated into curriculum. Each participant will take part in a variety of hands-on AIMS investigations to gain an understanding of such aspects as the scientific/mathematical content, classroom management, and connections with other curricular areas. *A Day with AIMS®* workshops may be offered anywhere in the United States. Necessary supplies and take-home materials are usually included in the enrollment fee.

A Week with AIMS®

Throughout the nation, AIMS offers many one-week workshops each year, usually in the summer. Each workshop lasts five days and includes at least 30 hours of AIMS hands-on instruction. Participants are grouped according to the grade level(s) in which they are interested. Instructors are members of the AIMS Instructional Leadership Network. Supplies for the activities and a generous supply of take-home materials are included in the enrollment fee. Sites are selected on the basis of applications submitted by educational organizations. If chosen to host a workshop, the host agency agrees to provide specified facilities and cooperate in the promotion of the workshop. The AIMS Education Foundation supplies workshop materials as well as the travel, housing, and meals for instructors.

AIMS One-Week Perspectives Workshops

Each summer, Fresno Pacific University offers AIMS one-week workshops on its campus in Fresno, California. AIMS Program Directors and highly qualified members of the AIMS National Leadership Network serve as instructors.

The AIMS Instructional Leadership Program

This is an AIMS staff-development program seeking to prepare facilitators for leadership roles in science/math education in their home districts or regions. Upon successful completion of the program, trained facilitators may become members of the AIMS Instructional Leadership Network, qualified to conduct AIMS workshops, teach AIMS in-service courses for college credit, and serve as AIMS consultants. Intensive training is provided in mathematics, science, process and thinking skills, workshop management, and other relevant topics.

College Credit and Grants

Those who participate in workshops may often qualify for college credit. If the workshop takes place on the campus of Fresno Pacific University, that institution may grant appropriate credit. If the workshop takes place off-campus, arrangements can sometimes be made for credit to be granted by another institution. In addition, the applicant's home school district is often willing to grant in-service or professional-development credit. Many educators who participate in AIMS workshops are recipients of various types of educational grants, either local or national. Nationally known foundations and funding agencies have long recognized the value of AIMS mathematics and science workshops to educators. The AIMS Education Foundation encourages educators interested in attending or hosting workshops to explore the possibilities suggested above. Although the Foundation strongly supports such interest, it reminds applicants that they have the primary responsibility for fulfilling *current* requirements.

For current information regarding the programs described above, please complete the following:

Information Request

Please send current information on the items checked:

___ *Basic Information Packet* on AIMS materials	___ *A Week with AIMS®* workshops
___ *AIMS Instructional Leadership Program*	___ Hosting information for *A Day with AIMS®* workshops
___ *AIMS One-Week Perspectives* workshops	___ Hosting information for *A Week with AIMS®* workshops

Name _____ Phone _____

Address _____

      Street   City   State   Zip

We invite you to subscribe to AIMS®!

Each issue of AIMS® contains a variety of material useful to educators at all grade levels. Feature articles of lasting value deal with topics such as mathematical or science concepts, curriculum, assessment, the teaching of process skills, and historical background. Several of the latest AIMS math/science investigations are always included, along with their reproducible activity sheets. As needs direct and space allows, various issues contain news of current developments, such as workshop schedules, activities of the AIMS Instructional Leadership Network, and announcements of upcoming publications.

AIMS® is published monthly, August through May. Subscriptions are on an annual basis only. A subscription entered at any time will begin with the next issue, but will also include the previous issues of that volume. Readers have preferred this arrangement because articles and activities within an annual volume are often interrelated.

Please note that an AIMS® subscription automatically includes duplication rights for one school site for all issues included in the subscription. Many schools build cost-effective library resources with their subscriptions.

YES! I am interested in subscribing to AIMS®.

Name _____   Home Phone _____

Address _____   City, State, Zip _____

Please send the following volumes (subject to availability):

_____	Volume VI	(1991-92)	$30.00	_____ Volume XI	(1996-97)	$30.00
_____	Volume VII	(1992-93)	$30.00	_____ Volume XII	(1997-98)	$30.00
_____	Volume VIII	(1993-94)	$30.00	_____ Volume XIII	(1998-99)	$30.00
_____	Volume IX	(1994-95)	$30.00	_____ Volume XIV	(1999-00)	$30.00
_____	Volume X	(1995-96)	$30.00	_____ Volume XV	(2000-01)	$30.00

_____ **Limited offer: Volumes XIV & XV (1999-2001) $55.00**
(Note: Prices may change without notice)

Check your method of payment:

☐ Check enclosed in the amount of $ _____

☐ Purchase order attached (Please include the P.O.#, the authorizing signature, and position of the authorizing person.)

☐ Credit Card   ☐ Visa   ☐ MasterCard   Amount $ _____

Card # _____   Expiration Date _____

Signature _____   Today's Date _____

Make checks payable to **AIMS Education Foundation.**
Mail to AIMS® Magazine, P.O. Box 8120, Fresno, CA 93747-8120.
Phone (559) 255-4094 or (888) 733-2467   FAX (559) 255-6396
AIMS Homepage: http://www.AIMSedu.org/

AIMS Program Publications

GRADES K-4 SERIES

Bats Incredible!
Brinca de Alegria Hacia la Primavera con las Matemáticas y Ciencias
Cáete de Gusto Hacia el Otoño con la Matemáticas y Ciencias
Cycles of Knowing and Growing
Fall Into Math and Science
Field Detectives
Glide Into Winter With Math and Science
Hardhatting in a Geo-World (Revised Edition, 1996)
Jaw Breakers and Heart Thumpers (Revised Edition, 1995)
Los Cincos Sentidos
Overhead and Underfoot (Revised Edition, 1994)
Patine al Invierno con Matemáticas y Ciencias
Popping With Power (Revised Edition, 1996)
Primariamente Física (Revised Edition, 1994)
Primarily Earth
Primariamente Plantas
Primarily Physics (Revised Edition, 1994)
Primarily Plants
Sense-able Science
Spring Into Math and Science
Under Construction

GRADES K-6 SERIES

Budding Botanist
Critters
El Botanista Principiante
Exploring Environments
Fabulous Fractions
Mostly Magnets
Ositos Nada Más
Primarily Bears
Principalmente Imanes
Water Precious Water

GRADES 5-9 SERIES

Actions with Fractions
Brick Layers
Brick Layers II
Conexiones Eléctricas
Down to Earth
Electrical Connections
Finding Your Bearings (Revised Edition, 1996)
Floaters and Sinkers (Revised Edition, 1995)
From Head to Toe
Fun With Foods
Gravity Rules!
Historical Connections in Mathematics, Volume I
Historical Connections in Mathematics, Volume II
Historical Connections in Mathematics, Volume III
Just for the Fun of It!
Machine Shop
Magnificent Microworld Adventures
Math + Science, A Solution
Off the Wall Science: A Poster Series Revisited
Our Wonderful World
Out of This World (Revised Edition, 1994)
Paper Square Geometry: The Mathematics of Origami
Pieces and Patterns, A Patchwork in Math and Science
Piezas y Diseños, un Mosaic de Matemáticas y Ciencias
Proportional Reasoning
Ray's Reflections
Soap Films and Bubbles
Spatial Visualization
The Sky's the Limit (Revised Edition, 1994)
The Amazing Circle, Volume 1
Through the Eyes of the Explorers:
    Minds-on Math & Mapping
What's Next, Volume 1
What's Next, Volume 2
What's Next, Volume 3

For further information write to:
AIMS Education Foundation • P.O. Box 8120 • Fresno, California 93747-8120
www.AIMSedu.org/ • Fax 559•255•6396

AIMS Duplication Rights Program

AIMS has received many requests from school districts for the purchase of unlimited duplication rights to AIMS materials. In response, the AIMS Education Foundation has formulated the program outlined below. There is a built-in flexibility which, we trust, will provide for those who use AIMS materials extensively to purchase such rights for either individual activities or entire books.

It is the goal of the AIMS Education Foundation to make its materials and programs available at reasonable cost. All income from the sale of publications and duplication rights is used to support AIMS programs; hence, strict adherence to regulations governing duplication is essential. Duplication of AIMS materials beyond limits set by copyright laws and those specified below is strictly forbidden.

Limited Duplication Rights

Any purchaser of an AIMS book may make up to *200 copies* of any activity in that book for use at *one school site*. Beyond that, rights must be purchased according to the appropriate category.

Unlimited Duplication Rights for Single Activities

An individual or school may purchase the right to make an unlimited number of copies of a single activity. The royalty is $5.00 per activity per school site.

Examples: 3 activities x 1 site x $5.00 = $15.00
9 activities x 3 sites x $5.00 = $135.00

Unlimited Duplication Rights for Entire Books

A school or district may purchase the right to make an unlimited number of copies of a single, *specified* book. The royalty is $20.00 per book per school site. This is in addition to the cost of the book.

Examples: 5 books x 1 site   x $20.00 = $100.00
12 books x 10 sites x $20.00 = $2400.00

Magazine/Newsletter Duplication Rights

Those who purchase *AIMS*® (magazine)/*Newsletter* are hereby granted permission to make up to 200 copies of any portion of it, provided these copies will be used for educational purposes.

Workshop Instructors' Duplication Rights

Workshop instructors may distribute to registered workshop participants a maximum of 100 copies of any article and/or 100 copies of no more than eight activities, provided these six conditions are met:

1. Since all AIMS activities are based upon the *AIMS Model of Mathematics* and the *AIMS Model of Learning*, leaders must include in their presentations an explanation of these two models.
2. Workshop instructors must relate the AIMS activities presented to these basic explanations of the AIMS philosophy of education.
3. The copyright notice must appear on all materials distributed.
4. Instructors must provide information enabling participants to order books and magazines from the Foundation.
5. Instructors must inform participants of their limited duplication rights as outlined below.
6. Only student pages may be duplicated.

Written permission must be obtained for duplication beyond the limits listed above. Additional royalty payments may be required.

Workshop Participants' Rights

Those enrolled in workshops in which AIMS student activity sheets are distributed may duplicate a maximum of 35 copies or enough to use the lessons one time with one class, whichever is less. Beyond that, rights must be purchased according to the appropriate category.

Application for Duplication Rights

The purchasing agency or individual must clearly specify the following:
1. Name, address, and telephone number
2. Titles of the books for Unlimited Duplication Rights contracts
3. Titles of activities for Unlimited Duplication Rights contracts
4. Names and addresses of school sites for which duplication rights are being purchased.

NOTE: Books to be duplicated must be purchased separately and are not included in the contract for Unlimited Duplication Rights.

The requested duplication rights are automatically authorized when proper payment is received, although a *Certificate of Duplication Rights* will be issued when the application is processed.

Address all correspondence to: **Contract Division**
AIMS Education Foundation
P.O. Box 8120
Fresno, CA 93747-8120

www.AIMSedu.org/
Fax 559•255•6396